Strong in the Grace

Other Books by Thomas Jones

Mind Change
The Overcomer's Handbook

God's Perfect Plan for Imperfect People
Paul's Letter to the Ephesians

Letters to New Disciples
*Practical Advice for Those Who Have
Decided to Follow Jesus*

No One Like Him
Jesus and His Message

To Live Is Christ
An Interactive Study of Philippians
(co-author)

The Prideful Soul's Guide to Humility
(co-author)

STRONG IN THE GRACE

Reclaiming the Heart of the Gospel

Thomas A. Jones

DPI
DISCIPLESHIP
PUBLICATIONS
INTERNATIONAL

Strong in the Grace
©2004 by Discipleship Publications International
2 Sterling Road, Billerica, Mass. 01862

Printed in the United States of America

Cover and interior design: Jennifer Matienzo

ISBN 1-57782-192-0

To my dear brother Gordon, who not only proclaims the grace of God, but who has shown it to me often.

Contents

Author's note: Though this book is first of all written to address specific issues in the fellowship of which I am a part, I believe the concerns discussed here can be found in various Christian communities. Most of the problems I am seeking to expose to Scriptural light are at least as old as the first century and have a way of making a comeback in every century.

HOPE FOR AN IMPERFECT PEOPLE

Several years ago I wrote an exposition of the Letter to the Ephesians, titled *God's Perfect Plan for Imperfect People*. In recent months because of events in our churches, some of us are more painfully aware than we have ever been that we are imperfect people. We have seen leaders in the church confessing sin and making apologies. We have seen unity strained and broken. We have seen some churches virtually collapse and have to begin rebuilding from the ground up. Such times are painful.

Those who go through these struggles must deal with the age-old issue of how God uses flawed human beings to accomplish his divine purposes. It is right to be stirred by the message that we can be part of something from God that makes an eternal difference in people's lives. But then we can feel such disappointment when we see failures in those who proclaimed these lofty ideas to us. Man's sin has a way of obliterating God's glory, and so we ask whether God was involved in our endeavor.

To understand what is happening, Biblical perspective is badly needed. Two thousand years ago Jesus came, born of a woman, born under the Jewish law. He was God incarnate. He was the fulfillment of a plan that had been unfolding for hundreds of years. God was in Christ. But our Bibles don't begin with Matthew or Mark or Luke or John. Thirty-nine books in our canon of Scripture were written before the birth of Jesus. The clear message was that God was working throughout all those years that led up to Jesus, but what was that history about? Do we find there story after story of righteous men and women who went from victory to victory? Do we find those who overcame all the temptations of the lower nature and always used money, power and influence in godly ways? Do we find a steady succession of leaders who led the nation of Israel to more and more righteous ends so that they finally produced a pristine temple and glorious people who were able to give the Son of God a hero's welcome?

This is not the Biblical story. From Genesis to Jesus, God was at work. Early on, he had a chosen people. He had a nation that was uniquely his. From generation to generation he was patiently working out a plan so that in "the fulness of time" (Galatians 4:4 KJV), he might send forth his Son. However, when we read through the Old Testament, we are struck not by the glory of Israel or the consistent faithfulness of her leaders, but by the flaws, the sin, the arrogance, the selfishness of both the people and the leaders. Are there heroes in the Old Testament? Absolutely, and Hebrews 11 describes many of them. But even these heroes like Noah, Abraham, Moses and Gideon were flawed and could easily have written their own letters of apology.

In 1 Samuel 4:21, the daughter-in-law of Eli the priest gave birth to a son, and the Scripture says, "She called the boy Ichabod, saying, 'The glory has departed from Israel....'" (Ichabod means "no glory.") A reader of the Jewish Scriptures prior to Jesus could have wondered if perhaps the whole nation shouldn't have been named Icabod. From Adam and Eve's sin to the shameful practice described in Malachi of offering God their leftovers and discards (Malachi 1:8), these were often a people of "no glory." But was God still at work? He was.

In 1 Corinthians 10 Paul reasons that in some terrible times described in the Old Testament, God was working to not only teach the people of that day, but to lay the groundwork for something more important. And then he makes this astounding statement:

> These things happened to them as examples and were written down as warnings for us, on whom the fulfillment of the ages has come. (1 Corinthians 10:11)

If we were only to look at Israel's failures and at God's discipline of them, we might just say, "Icabod—no glory." But Paul says God was at work so that something might be clear to us "on whom the fulfillment of the ages has come."

It seems to me there is a powerful truth here. As God works with his flawed and sinful people, what is happening at the moment may not be pretty, but the God who can work in all things for good has his eye not just on the present moment, but on fulfillment for the future. Even in some of the terrible times, God is working to get our attention and make us aware of deeper truths we have been missing.

As I was finishing up this small volume, I was also finishing the reading of Carl Sandburg's six-volume biography of Abraham Lincoln. As Lincoln was preparing to assume the presidency in 1860, a famous historian told him that the only way slavery would ever be brought to an end in the United States was through something as horrible as a great civil war. He was right. Sometimes great changes can come about only through something excruciatingly painful. I am one of many who have concluded that God is at work, showing us through the pain of recent months that there was something funda-mentally unsound about the emphasis in our message. My prayer is that this book will point us to the heart of God's healthy message and will help us to restore an emphasis on the gospel of God's grace.

> Even in some of the terrible times, God is working to get our attention and make us aware of deeper truths we have been missing.

You then, my son, be strong in the grace that is in Christ Jesus.

2 Timothy 2:1

See to it that no one misses the grace of God and that no bitter root grows up to cause trouble and defile many.

Hebrews 12:15

c h a p t e r   o n e

THE GOSPEL OF GOD'S GRACE: THE TRUNK OF THE TREE

> He [an elder] must hold firmly to the trustworthy
> message as it has been taught, so that he can
> encourage others by sound doctrine and refute
> those who oppose it.
>
> Titus 1:9

Leaders in God's church have many responsibilities, but none is higher than the responsibility of holding to and holding out the trustworthy message. Leadership in the kingdom of God is not just about good management or organization or decision-making; it is about implanting the core of God's message into the life of the church so that the church then holds out that message to the world. No church will ever be stronger than the message it proclaims. The message is what everything else is built upon.

Many readers of this book are the heirs of an emphasis on "restoration," and we have frequently heard calls to be a "restoration movement." In some cases in the past, the emphasis was focused on the proper form of church organization, the externals of worship, and on the way one responds to the gospel.

More recently some of us have been part of a movement that has focused on restoring commitment, Biblical relationships, and Biblical evangelism—all of which would seem to be more fundamental issues.

Yet, in both the earlier movement, which is now nearly two hundred years old, and in the more recent one, it would seem that there has been very little focus on restoring the gospel itself. That is the concern of this little book. *My contention is that the very core of the trustworthy message and the sound doctrine we are to hold to and hold out is the message of the grace of God that has been lavished on us in Christ (see Ephesians 1:7–8).*

As I write this, I am looking out at a wooded area behind my house. I can see trees that tower above me. Most of them have many limbs, and some of those are strong, thick and quite substantial; but all of those limbs are dependent on the trunk of the tree for life and existence. The theme of this book is that the gospel of God's grace is the trunk of the tree and that any effort to restore God's work in the world must begin with the greatest emphasis on this grace—the only hope of freedom from sin and fellowship with God.[1] We must take seriously Paul's charge to "be strong in the grace that is in Christ Jesus" (2 Timothy 2:1), or we will not be strong at all. Paul's statement most likely means "get your strength" from God's grace, but it could also refer to putting great emphasis on grace and taking a strong stand

> We must take seriously Paul's charge to "be strong in the grace that is in Christ Jesus," or we will not be strong at all.

---

[1] I should say here that a few of my fellow teachers have not been comfortable with this analogy. While agreeing with me that the gospel of God's grace is at the heart of the message, they are uncomfortable with the idea that it is the only trunk of the tree from which everything else grows. No analogy is perfect, and this one likely has its weaknesses, but I have received encouragement from other teachers to continue to use this metaphor as a way of pointing out the primacy of grace. I have just finished reading a book with a thesis that the cross of Christ is really at the

for it. Either way, it is clear that grace for Paul was central to Christian life and ministry.

Through the years I have seen, at various times, that churches I have been part of have been concerned to not leave out the grace of God and to make sure that this theme is at least included in our teaching. But it was as though it was being included as one of the limbs (and not always one of the most important ones). I have known very few who seemed passionate about showing that grace is the trunk of the tree or the very foundation of everything else. As we have studied the Bible with others in an evangelistic context, we have taken them carefully through a whole series of studies, but normally not one of these studies was focused on the message of grace and how we are saved by grace through faith. If those who were being studied with were paying close attention, they may have heard it mentioned, but it was hardly emphasized. I have sat in on studies with others when someone "counted the cost" with prospective disciples and then said at the end, "Of course, keep in mind, you are saved by grace." Other matters had been stressed and underlined,

core of the gospel. With such terminology I have no problem since in Scripture the message of the cross and the gospel of God's grace, while not identical, are inseparable and almost interchangeable.

with questions being asked to make sure the person "got it," but when it came to grace, it was almost an afterthought. As a consequence, many did not "get it."

Some years ago here in Boston, when I was teaching a large class of highly motivated Christians who had committed ten Saturdays in the fall to study the book of Hebrews, I surveyed the class on several topics. I discovered that nearly fifty percent of them did not have confidence in their salvation. Most of them had been in the church for some years, but they had little grasp of the message of grace. The writer of Hebrews said, "See to it that no one misses the grace of God" (Hebrews 12:15), but apparently, they had missed it. When we look at what we have studied with people and the sermons we have preached, it is not hard to see why. I am convinced that our failure to put the emphasis where the New Testament puts it has provided the soil that legalism could readily grow in. Our recent recognition that we too often descended into a mentality of performance and rule-keeping should also be a recognition that in many ways we are reaping what we have sown.

As the churches many of us are a part of have been through some trying times, we have recognized that God is disciplining us and calling us back to his path. There has been an increased concern for restoration. With a crisis in leadership and a recognition that we have followed some un-Biblical models in the area of leadership, there has been much concern to study the Scriptures about the role of elders, evangelists, teachers and deacons. This is certainly a right thing to do—but we must be sure our focus is on the heart and soul of the Biblical message.

Certainly, we must learn about other large and important limbs in the Christian tree, but it will all be in vain unless we give the proper place to the trunk. It will not be enough to "include" the message of God's grace as one topic among many and have it on a list of things we believe. It must truly become the core of our faith and the deepest conviction from which all else flows. It must become that which is consistently coming out in sermons, lessons and conversations. I want to challenge you to look carefully at the New Testament to see if the message of God's grace is really deserving of this emphasis. I want to call you to have the spirit of the Bereans and to see if the things I am saying are true (Acts 17:10–11). If you are a leader, I further want to challenge you to accept the role God calls you to play and ask you to see if the message of God's grace is the passion of your life.

When Paul wrote his letters to Timothy and Titus, he put a great deal of emphasis on what those in leadership roles were to teach (1 Timothy 1:3–5, 10–11; 3:2; 4:6, 11, 16; 6:3–4, 20; 2 Timothy 1:13; 2:1–2, 15, 24; 3:16–17; 4:1–5; Titus 1:9, 13; 2:1–11, 15). Again in Titus 1:9, regarding one who would serve as an elder and overseer of the church, Paul wrote: "He must hold firmly to the trustworthy message as it has been taught, so that he can encourage others by sound doctrine and refute those who oppose it." Paul has just described the tenor of life that we must see in an elder, but then he makes it clear that he must be more than a man with a certain character. *He must have a firm grip on the trustworthy message and must be able to build up the body of Christ with "sound doctrine."* That last phrase could be translated "healthy teaching." In these letters to young leaders, in which Paul speaks also of the way elders are to lead, what is the "sound doctrine"? What is the "healthy teaching"?

Growing up a "Restoration Movement" background in the middle of the twentieth century, I often heard the phrase "sound doctrine," but those who used it were almost always talking about the mostly external issues I mentioned at the beginning of this piece. But if we look carefully at the letter to Titus and then the letters to Timothy, what do we see as the core of the message for Paul?

To Titus he said, "You must teach what is in accord with sound doctrine" (Titus 2:1). This statement is followed by a group of instructions about what to teach to various groups in the church. Notice carefully Paul's words: "teach what is *in accord with* sound doctrine" (emphasis added). The word for "in accord with" is the Greek *prepo*. It means what is a "good fit with." In other words what follows in chapter 2 are some limbs of the tree that "fit with" or are "in accord with" the fundamentals of healthy teaching—that is, with the trunk of the tree.

After speaking of what is to be taught to the older and younger men and the older and younger women, Paul shows us his primary focus:

> For the grace of God that brings salvation has appeared to all men. It teaches us to say "No" to ungodliness and worldly passions, and to live self-controlled, upright and godly lives in this present age, while we wait for the blessed hope—the glorious appearing of our great God and Savior, Jesus

> Christ, who gave himself for us to redeem us from all wickedness and to purify for himself a people that are his very own, eager to do what is good.
>
> These, then, are the things you should teach. Encourage and rebuke with all authority. Do not let anyone despise you. (Titus 2:11–15)

The core of the message is "the grace of God that brings salvation." The grace of God is what then teaches us to say "No" to ungodliness and to live a different life. The other elements we are to learn grow out of grace. Grace is not simply another element, another thing on the list. It is the heart and soul of the message! If you miss this, you have missed it all. And what is the message of grace? It is that Jesus Christ gave himself for us to redeem us and purify us (vv13–14), and this is the basis—the only basis—for our salvation.

In chapter 3 of Titus, Paul will go into more detail as he describes the gospel:

> At one time we too were foolish, disobedient, deceived and enslaved by all kinds of passions and pleasures. We lived in malice and envy, being hated and hating one another. But when the kindness and love of God our Savior appeared, *he saved us, not because of righteous things we had done, but*

because of his mercy. He saved us through the washing of rebirth and renewal by the Holy Spirit, whom he poured out on us generously through Jesus Christ our Savior, so that, having been *justified by his grace,* we might become heirs having the hope of eternal life. *This is a trustworthy saying. And I want you to stress these things,* so that those who have trusted in God may be careful to devote themselves to doing what is good. These things are excellent and profitable for everyone. (Titus 3:3–8, emphasis added)

"This is a trustworthy saying." This is the "trustworthy message" in Titus 1:9 that the elders are to hold to and teach: we were lost; we were enslaved by our passions; but when the kindness—the extravagant generosity—of God appeared in Jesus Christ, he saved us. Our salvation is not in any way, big or small, a result of the righteous things we have done. It is entirely because of his mercy. The washing of rebirth and the renewal of the Holy Spirit came from his generosity, so we are clearly justified by grace. This is the good news! This is the gospel! This is what we must "stress" (v8—*diabebaioomai*—"affirm constantly"). It must become clear to all that this is the core of our message. This is what we must be known for above all else.

Paul's first letter to Timothy contains numerous imperatives. The young leader, elders and the church are called to adhere to God's standard in a variety of areas. If we are not careful, we could see 1 Timothy as a manual for the church that is just a list of "do's" and "don'ts." But we need to notice carefully in chapter 1 of the letter that Paul makes it clear what the heart of his message is (and watch again for our word "trustworthy"):

> I thank Christ Jesus our Lord, who has given me strength, that he considered me faithful, appointing me to his service. Even though I was once a blasphemer and a persecutor and a violent man, I was shown mercy because I acted in ignorance and unbelief. *The grace of our Lord was poured out on me abundantly,* along with the faith and love that are in Christ Jesus.
>
> *Here is a trustworthy saying that deserves full acceptance: Christ Jesus came into the world to save sinners—of whom I am the worst.* But for that very reason I was shown mercy so that in me, the worst of sinners, Christ Jesus might display his unlimited patience as an example for those who would believe on him and receive eternal life. Now to the King eternal, immortal, invisible, the only God, be honor

and glory for ever and ever. Amen. (1 Timothy
1:12–17, emphasis added)

Yes, Paul will give instructions in 1 Timothy on
a variety of issues, but his message is not just the
sum of those directives. The trustworthy message
is that Christ Jesus came into the world to save sinners and that the grace of our Lord has been
poured out on us abundantly. In the churches I
grew up in, there was much talk about sound doctrine, but there was little talk about grace. To Paul
this would represent the greatest contradiction.
The teaching about the abundant grace of God that
is poured out to us sinners is the sound and healthy
teaching. It is when churches or movements stray
from this that unhealthiness of all types begins to
come in.

When, sometime later, Paul wrote another letter to Timothy, he did not just cut to the chase and
begin to direct Timothy to do this or that. He did
exactly what he had told Titus to do: he stressed,
or continued to affirm, this message of God's
grace. Since he had made such a strong statement
in the first letter, we could understand if he had not
done so in the second, but this message was in the
very fabric of Paul's soul. Like Jeremiah, he could

not hold it in. Listen to more of his impassioned words:

> So do not be ashamed to testify about our Lord, or ashamed of me his prisoner. But join with me in suffering for the gospel, by the power of God, *who has saved us and called us to a holy life—not because of anything we have done but because of his own purpose and grace.* This grace was given us in Christ Jesus before the beginning of time, but it has now been revealed through the appearing of our Savior, Christ Jesus, who has destroyed death and has brought life and immortality to light through the gospel. *And of this gospel* I was appointed a herald and an apostle and a teacher. That is why I am suffering as I am. Yet I am not ashamed, because I know whom I have believed, and am convinced that he is able to guard what I have entrusted to him for that day.
>
> *What you heard from me, keep as the pattern of sound teaching,* with faith and love in Christ Jesus. Guard the good deposit that was entrusted to you— guard it with the help of the Holy Spirit who lives in us. (2 Timothy 1:8–14, emphasis added).

Paul is simply not going to take it for granted that Timothy will remember what the very basis of our life in Christ is. He will stress that we were saved and called to a holy and new life "not because of anything we have done but because of his own purpose and grace." At the end of this letter Paul will say he has fought the good fight, finished the race, and kept the faith. He also anticipates the crown of life that the Lord will give him, but he does not think for a minute that the crown will come because of anything he has done. As he said to the Corinthians: "By the grace of God I am what I am" (1 Corinthians 15:10).

And then he reminds his young leader, "What you heard from me, keep as the pattern of sound teaching" (1 Timothy 1:13). What was it that Timothy had heard as he traveled with Paul, as he was with Paul when he wrote to other churches, and what is it that he has heard from Paul in the two personal letters to him? Was it not the message that we are sinners saved only by the amazingly generous grace of God? Is that not the pattern of sound teaching that Timothy is to keep? And is it not the pattern we are to follow? Is this not the major message the church should hear from her leaders? Is this not the central message that the world should hear from the church? Is this not the message that children should hear from their

Christian parents?[2] But my concern here is not that we would get the wrong answer to a test question. I believe most all of us would say we are saved by grace, but is it the message we stress? Most of us have always had this teaching on a list of things that we believe. But I would insist that this is not enough and not in keeping with the weight the New Testament calls us to give this message. It must be more than one thing among many. We must be "strong" in the grace (2 Timothy 2:1). It must be obvious to all that, for us, it is the trunk of the tree. That means it deserves a lot more emphasis than many of us have given it.

When Paul wrote 1 and 2 Timothy and Titus, he was merely putting an exclamation mark on what he had written earlier in some of his best known letters. In both Romans and Ephesians, Paul goes to great lengths to discuss the grace of God before he turns to the things Christians should be doing. As some have put it, he first describes the "indicatives" before he turns to the "imperatives." Others have noted that "description" (what God has done) always comes before "prescription" (what we

---

[2] It is remarkable how similar this message is to that which the parents in ancient Israel were to bring to their children. See Deuteronomy 6:20–21.

should do). Paul obviously believes the actions of Christians need to come from being firmly rooted in the grace of God.

In Romans he basically spends eleven chapters showing that while we were sinners Christ died for us, that we are saved by a righteousness that comes from God, that God is for us, and that salvation does not depend on man but on God's mercy. Having written extensively about these themes that describe grace, he then says, "Therefore, I urge you, brothers, *in view of God's mercy,* to offer your bodies as living sacrifices, holy and pleasing to God—this is your spiritual act of worship" (Romans 12:1, emphasis added). At the heart of Paul's message was the grace and mercy of God, and he took great pains to make sure his hearers or readers had a clear view of both. He operates from the conviction that once we see God's grace and take our stand in it, then we are prepared to act.

We see this same pattern in Ephesians in which he spends the first half of the letter focusing on what God has done, showing that salvation is by grace through faith and not of ourselves (Ephesians 2:8–10). Only then is he ready to write the second half and say, "As a prisoner for the Lord, then, I urge you to live a life worthy of the calling you have received" (Ephesians 4:1). Indicative before imperative. Description before prescription.

In Galatians we do not have the systematic approach we find in Romans and Ephesians, but rather a visceral reaction to the fact that the Christians there are turning to another gospel that is no gospel at all because it focuses on human effort and not on the grace of God. Paul starts the letter on this note and continues this emphasis to the end where he says, "May I never boast except in the cross of our Lord Jesus Christ" (Galatians 6:14). There is no doubt from reading these letters that the gospel of God's grace was the heart of Paul's message.

Some, most likely, will feel that having this emphasis will mean that our message will not be distinct. After all, don't a lot of other groups put great emphasis on God's grace? I would hope that one of the lessons we are learning is that our goal is not to be distinct.[3] Our goal is to be faithful and to handle correctly the word of truth. Our goal is not to create a unique and separate fellowship that stands above others or boasts of anything we have done. Our goal must be to hold to and to hold out

---

[3] Jesus' disciples had some things to learn about how wrong-headed their efforts to be distinct were (Mark 9:38–40).

31

the trustworthy message *and then see what God does.* If in our faithfulness God makes us distinct or if God brings us more into fellowship with others, may the name of God be praised. But may we be content to just keep the pattern of sound teaching, preach the trustworthy message, and testify about our Lord. Our calling is not to be different from others, or God forbid, better than others. Our calling is to "be strong in the grace that is in Christ Jesus" (2 Timothy 2:1).

The Word became flesh and made his dwelling among us. We have seen his glory, the glory of the One and Only, who came from the Father, full of grace and truth.

John testifies concerning him. He cries out, saying, "This was he of whom I said, 'He who comes after me has surpassed me because he was before me.'" From the fullness of his grace we have all received one blessing after another. For the law was given through Moses; grace and truth came through Jesus Christ.

John 1:14–17

THE MESSAGE OF JESUS

S ome of you have no doubt noticed how I have so far primarily focused on the writings of Paul. But as we have looked at what Paul stresses, you may have wondered if we see the same emphasis in Jesus. You may have even thought that you see something else in Jesus, particularly when you consider the call to discipleship that he gave and the hard-hitting teachings of the Sermon on the Mount. After all, you might note, Jesus never even used the word "grace," so how can we say this was at the heart of his message?

First of all, keep in mind that there are many other messages in Paul's writings as well. He had plenty of hard-hitting things to say and plenty of strong challenges for Christians. I am not suggesting for a moment that Paul preached nothing else but the abundant grace and love of God. I am saying as strongly as I know how to say it that grace was the heart and soul of his message and this is the message his letters tell us to put at the very center of our teaching. It will not be the only thing we teach, but it should be the foundation on which everything else is built. It must be the lens through which we look to examine any other subject. With this centrality of focus in mind, look at the first recorded words of Jesus as he begins his ministry:

> "The time has come," he said. "The kingdom of God is near. Repent and believe the good news!" (Mark 1:15)

For our purposes, I will not take the time to say more about this verse. For a more detailed study I would refer you to chapter 6 ("The Kingdom of God") and chapter 7 ("Extravagant Generosity") in my book *No One Like Him: Jesus and His Message.*[1] But here is what we can say: at the heart of Jesus' message was the announcement of "good news," and the basic call was to repent (to turn, to change) and to believe (to trust, to rely on, to build on) this good news. From the very outset, Jesus was saying in so many words, "The kingdom of God is breaking

---

[1] Thomas Jones, *No One Like Him* (Billerica, Mass: Discipleship Publications International, 2002).

in; the goodness of the age to come is breaking into this age, and you need to trust and embrace this truth." His message was not, "You need to repent and pull yourselves up by your own bootstraps." That is what they were already trying to do. His message was, "You need to change and trust the good news of what God is bringing to you."

In Matthew's account we see that it is not long after this that Jesus preaches the Sermon on the Mount. His message there has been looked at in dozens of different ways by everyone from Augustine to Jefferson to Tolstoy to Ghandi. What I think often gets overlooked is the very first statement of the sermon, in which we get the same message that we get in all of Paul's letters—and indeed the whole of the New Testament.

Jesus begins by saying, "Blessed are the poor in spirit, for theirs is the kingdom of heaven" (Matthew 5:3). Who is it that will inherit the blessings of the kingdom? Who is it that will be received by God, affirmed by God and justified by God? Is it that person who works hard to earn his salvation and who then can be proud and thankful for his accomplishments? Is it the person who will memorize the rest of the Sermon on the Mount and then keep every detail? No, it is the person who is fully in touch with the fact that he is in the greatest of need and comes to God humbly for the salvation that he can never earn.

There were two words in the Greek language for "poor" that Jesus could have used in this statement. One meant that you were a working person who had nothing extra. The other meant that you were so poor that you had to beg. Jesus would have spoken Aramaic, but when Matthew translates what Jesus said into Greek, he uses the second word. Jesus is saying, "Those who are going to be blessed by God are those who realize that they are spiritual beggars and that they could never save themselves." (And by the way, the rest of the Sermon on the Mount has a way of humbling us all and bringing us back to this first beatitude again and again.) When we don't miss it, the first words of the Sermon on the Mount are a declaration of the gospel: the good news of salvation by grace through faith. When Paul writes what we considered earlier ("Christ Jesus came into the world to save sinners—of whom I am the worst"), he was living out the first beatitude. No, Paul did not preach a message different from that of Jesus. Certainly, after the death, burial and resurrection of Jesus, it was possible to preach the message even more clearly, but it was the same message.

In the "Parable of the Pharisee and the Tax Collector," Jesus shows that the person who is justified before God is the one who says, "God, have mercy on me, a sinner," and not the diligent rule-keeper who prided himself on his goodness (Luke 18:9–14). The man who looked the religious part but trusted in himself ("I

> The apostles of Jesus, who faithfully bore witness to him, put the greatest emphasis on the grace of God because they had learned it from Jesus and experienced it in their relationship with him.

thank you Lord that I...") went home separated from God with nothing but temporary human praise to show for all his efforts. The disreputable man who saw his need and was poor in spirit, amazingly went home finding favor with God and being justified before him.

The "Parable of the Unforgiving Servant" shows us that we are all hopelessly and pathetically lost without God's grace and mercy (Matthew 18:

STRONG IN THE GRACE

23–35), in addition to showing us that this mercy must be passed on to others, lest we lose it ourselves.

But then no parable more clearly shows Jesus' emphasis on God's extravagant generosity than the one we know as the "Parable of the Prodigal Son" (Luke 15:11–32). The erring son did nothing to deserve it, but he received grace and forgiveness from the father who ran to meet him and gave him blessing upon blessing. Read the parable and then read Paul's words in Ephesians 1:7–8: "In him we have redemption through his blood, the forgiveness of sins, in accordance with the *riches of God's grace* that he *lavished on us* with all wisdom and understanding"[2] —and you see again that Paul and Jesus preached the same message. Though the Gospel writers do not tell us of Jesus using the word "grace," the message of salvation and relationship with God by grace is everywhere in Jesus' teaching.

Perhaps no actual incident in Jesus' life shows how grace was at the center of his teaching more than the story of the woman taken in the act of adultery (John 8). I will repeat here a description of this story that is found in *No One Like Him*:

[2] Emphasis added.

The account finds Jesus in Jerusalem at one of those times only mentioned by John. It appears that it was about six months before Jesus would come back there for the Passover and the final events of his life. After a night camped out on the Mount of Olives, Jesus rose early and made his way to the temple courts where he found an opportunity to teach and discuss the good news of the kingdom. A rude interruption by the Pharisees and teachers of the law gave him the opportunity to illustrate what it was all about.

The local "morals police" had apparently been keeping watch on people's lives, or perhaps, more odiously, setting a trap for a victim. At any rate, these religious teachers come into Jesus' meeting with a woman whom they say was caught in adultery. Since the man involved is nowhere to be seen, we might suspect that he escaped. More likely, he was just a part of the trap that had been set, since the entire situation was being orchestrated to discredit Jesus. Obviously, these teachers knew that they didn't need an opinion from an itinerate preacher from Galilee. The day before, they had made enough fun of where he was from (John 7:52).

With their motives obviously transparent, the Pharisees pressed on to ask how Jesus would rule in this case.

They reminded him that the Law of Moses required stoning, and they wanted to know what he would say. There was something of a bluff here, since the Jews could no longer carry out capital punishment. Only the Roman procurator could enforce that, and he was not likely to approve something of this nature.

What Jesus did next is enigmatic. He stooped down and began writing on the ground with his finger. We have no idea what he wrote; but whatever he wrote, it did not stop the challenges. What he said next, however, did have impact: "If any one of you is without sin, let him be the first to throw a stone at her" (John 8:7). After more writing on the ground, he looked up to see the crowd of accusers drifting away until the last was gone. With no one left to charge her, the legal case was over. John ends the account with these words:

> Jesus straightened up and asked her, "Woman, where are they? Has no one condemned you?"

"No one, sir," she said.

"Then neither do I condemn you," Jesus
declared. "Go now and leave your life of sin."
(John 8:10–11)

God's extravagant generosity did not just make
a good story like the one in Luke 15. Jesus did
not just preach it. He put it into practice in real
life. Jesus did not ignore the fact that the woman
had her own culpability, but he showed her that
there was at least one man and the one God who
could offer her forgiveness and a fresh start. She
may have been a prostitute. John does not say,
but from the references in Matthew 21 and the
story in Luke 7, we know that some with that
background were coming to Jesus and to the
kingdom. Whatever her story, she had to have
left this experience understanding that God is
amazingly generous and full of grace. The religious police did not condemn her that day—
they just wandered off. Jesus, on the other hand,
looked her in the face and clearly communicat-
ed, "I don't condemn you." I doubt she ever forgot those words. No condemnation![3]

[3] Jones, *No One Like Him*, 90–92.

The apostles of Jesus, who faithfully bore witness to him, put the greatest emphasis on the grace of God because they had learned it from Jesus and experienced it in their relationship with him. Men like Peter and Paul had personally sinned and felt his grace and forgiveness. They knew they would have had no standing with God without that grace and forgiveness. They knew that the good news of the kingdom that Jesus preached was not the good news that you can be under a new law or follow better rules. They knew that the good news was that the grace of God is breaking into this present age, and we can all share in it.

"All the prophets testify about him that everyone who believes in him receives forgiveness of sins through his name."

Acts 10:43

Therefore, since we have been justified through faith, we have peace with God through our Lord Jesus Christ, through whom we have gained access by faith into this grace in which we now stand. And we rejoice in the hope of the glory of God.

Romans 5:1–2

For it is by grace you have been saved, through faith—and this not from yourselves, it is the gift of God—not by works, so that no one can boast. For we are God's workmanship, created in Christ Jesus to do good works, which God prepared in advance for us to do.

Ephesians 2:8–10

c h a p t e r   t h r e e

BY GRACE THROUGH FAITH

Preaching the gospel, of course, will be in vain if we do not make it clear how to respond to the gospel. The gospel has power in people's lives only when it is received. God has made us an offer full of grace, but we must accept the offer. Therefore, a crucial element of the trustworthy message must be the clear Biblical word of how to receive and accept God's gracious offer of forgiveness, redemption and new life.

If we try hard not to be shaped by tradition or by reaction, and we just go the New Testament seeking the key element in the response to the gospel, there is one dominant word that emerges. That word is "faith"—or its verb form "believe." There are 472 occurrences of the word "faith" or a form of the words "trust" or "believe" in the New Testament. This is an astounding number. Compare that to 200 references to "love," 75 references to "hope," 64 references to some form of the word "baptize," 68 references to some form of the word "obey," and 52 references to some form of the word "repent." Of course, it is only by examining some of the key texts that we see the significance of faith, but the sheer number of references shows us this was the primary element in the response to the good news. But I would suggest that in fellowships I have been part of, this has not been an element that has received primary emphasis. In the same way that we have often made too quick an assumption about grace and moved on to other things, we have often assumed faith and moved on. A serious effort to restore the Biblical emphasis on the gospel must include a serious effort to restore the primacy of faith.

A look at the following passages (most of which describe the connection of faith to salvation) shows the central role of faith in our response to the gospel. I would encourage you to read each one and skip none of them in order to get the full impact:[1]

---

[1] Emphasis added on all of the following references.

Mark 1:15

"The time has come," he said. "The kingdom of God is near. Repent and *believe the good news!*"

John 1:12

Yet to all who received him, to those *who believed in his name,* he gave the right to become children of God—

John 3:14–16

"Just as Moses lifted up the snake in the desert, so the Son of Man must be lifted up, that everyone who *believes in him* may have eternal life.

"For God so loved the world that he gave his one and only Son, that whoever *believes in him* shall not perish but have eternal life."

John 3:18

"*Whoever believes in him* is not condemned, but whoever does not believe stands condemned already because he has not believed in the name of God's one and only Son."

John 3:36

"*Whoever believes in the Son* has eternal life, but whoever rejects the Son will not see life, for God's wrath remains on him."

John 5:24

"I tell you the truth, whoever hears my word and *believes him who sent me* has eternal life and will not be condemned; he has crossed over from death to life."

John 6:28–29

Then they asked him, "What must we do to do the works God requires?"

Jesus answered, *"The work of God is this: to believe in the one he has sent."*

John 6:35

Then Jesus declared, "I am the bread of life. He who comes to me will never go hungry, and he *who believes in me* will never be thirsty."

John 6:40

"For my Father's will is that everyone who looks to the Son and *believes in him* shall have eternal life, and I will raise him up at the last day."

John 6:47

"I tell you the truth, he *who believes* has everlasting life."

John 7:38

"*Whoever believes in me,* as the Scripture has said, streams of living water will flow from within him."

John 10:42

And in that place *many believed* in Jesus.

John 11:25–26

Jesus said to her, "I am the resurrection and the life. He *who believes in me* will live, even though he dies; and whoever lives and *believes in me* will never die. Do you believe this?"

Acts 4:4

But many who heard the message *believed,* and the number of men grew to about five thousand.

Acts 5:14

Nevertheless, more and more men and women *believed in the Lord* and were added to their number.

Acts 10:43

"All the prophets testify about him that everyone *who believes in him* receives forgiveness of sins through his name."

Acts 11:21

The Lord's hand was with them, and a great number of people *believed* and turned to the Lord.

Acts 13:48

When the Gentiles heard this, they were glad and honored the word of the Lord; and all who were appointed for eternal life *believed*.

Acts 15:7

After much discussion, Peter got up and addressed them: "Brothers, you know that some time ago God made a choice among you that the Gentiles *might hear from my lips the message of the gospel and believe*."

Acts 16:31

They replied, "*Believe in the Lord Jesus,* and you will be saved—you and your household."

Acts 17:12

Many of the Jews *believed*, as did also a number of prominent Greek women and many Greek men.

Acts 18:8

Crispus, the synagogue ruler, and his entire household believed in the Lord; and many of the

Corinthians who heard him *believed* and were baptized.

Acts 20:21

I have declared to both Jews and Greeks that they must turn to God in repentance and *have faith in our Lord Jesus.*

Acts 26:17–18

[Jesus to Paul] "I will rescue you from your own people and from the Gentiles. I am sending you to them to open their eyes and turn them from darkness to light, and from the power of Satan to God, so that they may receive forgiveness of sins and a place among those who are *sanctified by faith* in me."

Romans 3:22

This righteousness from God *comes through faith* in Jesus Christ to all who believe. There is no difference….

Romans 3:26

…he did it to demonstrate his justice at the present time, so as to be just and the one who justifies those *who have faith* in Jesus.

Romans 3:28

For we maintain that a man is *justified by faith* apart from observing the law.

Romans 4:5

However, to the man who does not work but *trusts* God who justifies the wicked, his *faith* is credited as righteousness.

Romans 5:1–2

Therefore, since we have been *justified through faith,* we have peace with God through our Lord Jesus Christ, through whom we have *gained access by faith* into this grace in which we now stand. And we rejoice in the hope of the glory of God.

Galatians 2:16

…know that a man is not justified by observing the law, *but by faith* in Jesus Christ. So we, too, have *put our faith* in Christ Jesus that we may be *justified by faith* in Christ and not by observing the law, because by observing the law no one will be justified.

Galatians 3:11

Clearly no one is justified before God by the law, because, *"The righteous will live by faith."*

Galatians 3:24

So the law was put in charge to lead us to Christ that we might be *justified by faith*.

Ephesians 2:8

For it is *by grace you have been saved, through faith*—and this not from yourselves, it is the gift of God—

Philippians 3:7–9

But whatever was to my profit I now consider loss for the sake of Christ. What is more, I consider everything a loss compared to the surpassing greatness of knowing Christ Jesus my Lord, for whose sake I have lost all things. I consider them rubbish, that I may gain Christ and be found in him, not having a righteousness of my own that comes from the law, but that *which is through faith in Christ*—the righteousness that comes from God and is by faith.

In these more than thirty texts from the Gospels, Acts and the Letters, we see that the primary God-ordained response to the grace that comes through Christ is faith. Salvation and eternal life come through believing in Jesus. The Greek word for "believe" is the word *pisteo,* and the word for "faith" is the word *pistis*. Almost all scholars emphasize that both words mean more than intellectual belief. They carry with them the idea of trust. Thus, what enables us to receive the grace of God and what justifies us in his sight is our trust in and our reliance on what he has done in Jesus Christ. We repent—we turn away from trusting ourselves and trusting our righteousness and trusting our performance—and we believe, that is, we put our trust in the righteousness of Christ. No passage describes this more powerfully than the previous one from Philippians 3. It is the complete trust in Christ that saves and justifies us.

The difference between intellectual assent (mere belief) and trust has often been well illustrated by the story of the man who was skilled at walking a tightrope. He made the claim that he could roll a barrel with a man in it across Niagara Falls on the tightrope. We see *belief* in the people who say, "We believe you can do it." We see *trust* in the man who is willing to get in the barrel! Faith in Jesus, as the Bible describes it, is not just believing he did the things he claimed; it is putting the weight of your life down on that belief. It is living your life based on that confidence. It is giving up trying to be good enough, and instead, trusting that in Christ and through his atoning sacrifice, you have been brought to God "without blemish" and are now "free from accusation" (Colossians 1:22).

Sadly, in our effort to supply what may be missing in the evangelistic preaching of other groups, some of us have put too little emphasis on this monumental aspect of our response to the gospel. My fear, justified by much experience, is that far too many people make a response to the gospel that is genuine, but is still full of self-effort. They do not realize that the first and foremost and primary thing they must do is to stop trusting their own efforts and to trust completely in what Christ has done for them. Or if they do this at the beginning, it is not long before they begin to rely once more on their own resources (in a church culture in which we have emphasized performance), following in the steps of the Galatians to whom Paul wrote these words:

> A serious effort to restore the Biblical emphasis on the gospel must include a serious effort to restore the primacy of faith.

> Are you so foolish? After beginning with the Spirit, are you now trying to attain your goal by human effort? (Galatians 3:3)

I would suggest that with any approach to studying the Bible with others that we not only need to give the greatest emphasis to the gospel of God's grace, but that we operate with a conviction that every person needs to be taught what it means to trust and rely on this grace. Helping every person to understand *justification by grace through faith* must be a top priority. Sadly, I believe that many people do not have this understanding. They believe that it is how well they are doing spiritually, how consistent they are with quiet times or how much they are sharing their faith that justifies them before God—so that the spiritual security that they feel goes up and down as their performance goes up and down.

Several years ago I had the opportunity to study the Bible with a man who lived much of his life enslaved to a spiritual performance model, always trying to do enough but always feeling guilty that he had failed. He had often read the Bible and attended many activities where it was discussed, but in the words of Hebrews 12, he had missed the grace of God. Discouraged by his belief that he could never measure up, he had finally given up and pulled away from any Christian community. As we studied in depth the message of God's grace, hope returned. The night he was baptized into Christ, I added a third question to the two that many of us often ask just prior to a baptism. I said, "Tom, do you tonight put all your trust in the righteousness of Christ and in the grace that comes through him, and not in your own righteousness?" My belief is that it would not be a bad idea for us to routinely ask that same question of others.

A special friend, and one well-schooled in the Scriptures, read one of the last drafts of this book and shared with me a thought that I want to pass on to you. He encouraged me to add to this chapter that our faith in God's grace needs to be a response that comes from deep gratitude for what God in Christ has done for us. His words are on target. Trusting God's grace should never be seen as something we "have to do," but rather as what we get to do in view of such amazingly gracious things done for us. Our faith should come from a profoundly grateful heart.

As I thought about my friend's input, another thought came to me. Trusting God is not a type of legal transaction in which you fulfill a technicality that changes your status. This is all about a God who is seeking a relationship with us, and at the heart of any relationship is trust. Faith then is not the new or more simplified legal requirement to replace a host of other requirements. Faith is the essence of a relationship. Our fellowship with God is created when we, from our hearts, show both gratitude for and confidence in God's grace, and put our trust in him, his sacrificial action taken for us and his plan for our lives. Thus we are justified and reconciled by grace through faith—a faith in Jesus as Lord which we will joyfully confess (Romans 10:9–10).

If the grace of God is the heart of the gospel, then trusting, having faith in that grace, is the heart of the response to the gospel. There is more to say about the response, but the emphasis that is most needed is trusting (or fully accepting) grace. Once we have laid the most solid foundation of faith and trust, then we can show how repentance and baptism grow out of that foundation—or in the case of repentance, may even lead to faith and trust.

And so John came, baptizing in the desert region and preaching a baptism of repentance for the forgiveness of sins.

Mark 1:4

"Therefore let all Israel be assured of this: God has made this Jesus, whom you crucified, both Lord and Christ."

When the people heard this, they were cut to the heart and said to Peter and the other apostles, "Brothers, what shall we do?"

Peter replied, "Repent and be baptized, every one of you, in the name of Jesus Christ for the forgiveness of your sins. And you will receive the gift of the Holy Spirit."

Acts 2:36–38

You are all sons of God through faith in Christ Jesus, for all of you who were baptized into Christ have clothed yourselves with Christ.

Galatians 3:26–27

c h a p t e r   f o u r

REPENTANCE AND BAPTISM

There are various theological schools that would say that having talked about grace and faith, we have said all that needs to be said about the gospel and how to respond to it. This, however, is where we need to keep reading Scripture and where we need to keep listening.

Repentance

In the earliest Christian sermon, Peter's response to his convicted hearers was "Repent and be baptized, every one of you, in the name of Jesus Christ for the forgiveness of your sins" (Acts 2:38). Repentance was certainly a key element in the response to the gospel of God. In his ministry Jesus had spoken often of repentance: "I have not come to call the righteous, but sinners to repentance" (Luke 5:32). His words later in Luke could not be more pointed or show more clearly how essential repentance is:

> Now there were some present at that time who told Jesus about the Galileans whose blood Pilate had mixed with their sacrifices. Jesus answered, "Do you think that these Galileans were worse sinners than all the other Galileans because they suffered this way? I tell you, no! But *unless you repent, you too will all perish.* Or those eighteen who died when the tower in Siloam fell on them—do you think they were more guilty than all the others living in Jerusalem? I tell you, no! *But unless you repent, you too will all perish.*" (Luke 13:1–5, emphasis added)

Genuine faith, that is, a genuine desire to stop trusting one's own efforts and to start relying on God, will always lead to repentance. In fact, it might be argued that this is repentance. The Greek word for repentance is *metanoia*, and it is all about "turning your mind." When faith is real, repentance will follow, and this is what we see in Acts 2 as a great number respond. If you have decided to change everything about what you are trusting, a new direction of life will come next, as surely as day follows night.

It is in the preaching of John the Baptist that we first hear the connection of repentance and forgiveness of sin, as John's baptism is described as "a baptism of repentance for the forgiveness of sins" (Mark 1:4). The resurrected Christ would later emphasize this connection, as Luke reports at the end of his Gospel:

> He told them, "This is what is written: The Christ will suffer and rise from the dead on the third day, and *repentance and forgiveness of sins* will be preached in his name to all nations, beginning at Jerusalem." (Luke 24:46–47, emphasis added)

It is not surprising then to read from the same Luke that the crowds on the day of Pentecost, nearly fifty days later, were told that they must "repent and be baptized...in the name of Jesus Christ for the forgiveness of [their] sins" (Acts 2:38). While there may not be another statement this clear in the rest of the book of Acts, the material Luke presents shows us that repentance was continually connected with forgiveness and justification. In another sermon sometime later, Peter proclaims:

> "Repent, then, and turn to God, so that your sins may be wiped out, that times of refreshing may come from the Lord...." (Acts 3:19)

And then later he preached,

> "God exalted him to his own right hand as Prince and Savior that he might give repentance and forgiveness of sins to Israel." (Acts 5:31)

After understanding that the Gentiles had been given the grace of God just as the Jews had, the disciples responded, "So then, God has granted even the Gentiles repentance unto life" (Acts 11:18). Later to the elders at Ephesus, Paul would report, "I have declared to both Jews and Greeks that they must turn to God in repentance and have faith in our Lord Jesus" (Acts 20:21). It is interesting how here, as in Jesus' first statement about repentance, it comes before faith. However you understand this, we must see that there is an intimate connection between the two. True faith will lead to repentance. But repentance, that is, turning away from our self-trust and self-focus, allows us to put our faith completely in Christ.

When Martin Luther rediscovered the Biblical idea of justification by faith (and we can be thankful for his work), he unfortunately translated Romans 1:17: "The righteous live by faith *alone*." One of his famous dictums was "*sola fide*"—faith alone. Eventually a whole body of theology was built from this that still affects millions today. There are two problems with Luther's statement: (1) While we can be most sympathetic and supportive of what Luther wanted to emphasize, the word "alone" is not in the text, and nowhere does the Scripture say we are justified or that we live by faith *alone*. (2) The deeper problem is that *Biblical faith is never alone*. Biblical faith is intimately connected to repentance (which is

> Taking hold of one sleeve of his jacket and turning it inside out and back again, he said, "In the New Testament, faith and baptism are the inside and outside of the same thing."

then intimately connected to obedience—see Romans 1:5). You simply cannot find faith in Jesus that is without repentance.

Baptism

Perhaps if we were writing a spiritual book to emphasize justification by faith, we would want to make sure that there was no physical act involved with the process of making a connection to God.

We might reason that spirituality is all about what goes on in the head and in the heart and is not to be tied in any way to an outward action. But when we examine the New Testament, this is not what we find. The same people who exalt the role of faith and teach that justification is by faith and not by works, also call all men to respond to the good news of God's grace by being baptized (immersed) in the name of Jesus.

When we looked at repentance, we saw that baptism was also called for in that first Christian sermon in Acts 2. We see that it was for the forgiveness of sins (v38) and that the preaching of the gospel throughout Acts always included the call to baptism. Luke tells us that Philip the evangelist told the Ethiopian "the good news about Jesus," after which the Ethiopian responded, "Look, here is water. Why shouldn't I be baptized?" (Acts 8:35–36). Philip's preaching of the good news about Jesus would have included the call to baptism. Having declared his desire, both Philip and the man went down into the water and he was baptized (v38).

In Acts we find baptism consistently called for. We find it connected with salvation. But since it is being preached, at least later on in the book, by the leading spokesman for justification by faith, we know it is not being seen as a good work that earns us God's forgiveness. Instead, it is seen, as is repentance, as an expression of faith. If all we had was the book of Acts, we would still know that baptism was a part of our response to the gospel, but it is in the letters that we learn the deeper significance of baptism and how it is so intimately linked with faith.

In Romans, Galatians, Ephesians and Colossians, all letters that put the greatest of emphasis on justification by grace through faith, Paul includes references to baptism. Each of these references describes baptism into Christ as a critical point in the life of a disciple. Let's look at an example from each letter.

Romans 6:1–5

> What shall we say, then? Shall we go on sinning so that grace may increase? By no means! We died to sin; how can we live in it any longer? Or don't you know that all of us who were baptized into Christ Jesus were baptized into his death? We were therefore buried with him through baptism into death in order that, just as Christ was raised from the dead through the glory of the Father, we too may live a new life.

69

If we have been united with him like this in his death, we will certainly also be united with him in his resurrection.

Having shown in the first five chapters of Romans that we are saved by grace through faith, Paul is aware of the charge that some will make that this assertion allows people to sin any way they want to. He has probably been accused of letting people go to this point. As he gives his response to this idea, he reminds his readers that when they put their faith in the gospel of Christ, they were baptized and in that baptism, they were baptized into his death. They were united with his death, with his burial and then, most gloriously, with his resurrection. When Paul wants to take them back to the moment in time when they died and when they were resurrected, he takes them back to baptism. That is where they fully expressed that they were ready to trust the grace of Christ and not their own works.

Galatians 3:26–28

You are all sons of God through faith in Christ Jesus, for all of you who were baptized into Christ have clothed yourselves with Christ. There is neither Jew

nor Greek, slave nor free, male nor female, for you
are all one in Christ Jesus.

Once again, we have a passage that is written in
the midst of the strongest possible defense of justification by faith. The letter to the Galatians was written for one overwhelming reason: the Galatian disciples were leaving the grace model and returning to
a performance model. This is seen so clearly at the
beginning of chapter 3 when Paul writes,

You foolish Galatians! Who has bewitched you?
Before your very eyes Jesus Christ was clearly por-
trayed as crucified. I would like to learn just one thing
from you: Did you receive the Spirit by observing the
law, or *by believing what you heard*? Are you so foolish? After beginning with the Spirit, are you now trying to *attain your goal by human effort*? (Galatians
3:1–3, emphasis added)

But in the midst of this strong call to trust grace,
not our performance, Paul refers the Galatians to
baptism. If Paul had in any way thought that baptism was some meritorious work that we can boast
about, he never would have mentioned it as he does
here. But it is obvious that Paul saw, again as in
Romans, that the moment of baptism was a "turning point" for them. And in Galatians 3:26–27 it is so

important to see the link between faith and baptism: "You are all sons of God through faith in Christ Jesus." This was his theme in Galatians as it was in his whole life. But the man who deeply believes this can say, "For all of you who have been baptized into Christ have clothed yourselves with Christ."

Thirty years ago, I attended a symposium conducted by G. R. Beasley-Murray, one the leading New Testament scholars of the last half century. Some years earlier he had written the definitive work on baptism, *Baptism in the New Testament*.[1] I will always remember an illustration that he used when he spoke about Galatians 3:26–27. Taking hold of one sleeve of his jacket and turning it inside out and back again, he said, "In the New Testament, faith and baptism are the inside and outside of the same thing." His point was that when a person is baptized into Christ, that person is just expressing his or her faith or trust in Christ Jesus, and this is why Paul saw no problem in putting emphasis on it in a letter wholly devoted to salvation by grace through faith.

Through the years I have heard teaching that makes it sound as if faith, repentance and baptism

[1] G. R. Beasley-Murray, *Baptism in the New Testament* (Grand Rapids: Eerdmans, 1962).

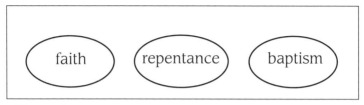

Figure 1

are three distinct elements, as in step one, step two and step three. (See figure 1.) Biblically I would suggest that the three are better thought of as you see in figure 2, which illustrates that repentance and baptism are part and parcel of the response of faith.

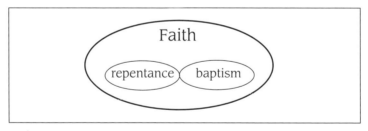

Figure 2

Ephesians 4:4–6

There is one body and one Spirit—just as you were called to one hope when you were called—one Lord, one faith, one baptism; one God and Father of all, who is over all and through all and in all.

73

We can certainly agree that baptism is not mentioned very often in the Letters and that it is certainly not talked about as often as faith. However, when baptism does show up, it shows up in crucial places. This is certainly true here. Again, we are in the midst of a letter that is stressing that salvation is not by works but is by faith. Paul could not have been clearer about this than he was in Ephesians 2:

> For it is by grace you have been saved, through faith—and this not from yourselves, it is the gift of God—not by works, so that no one can boast. (Ephesians 2:8–9)

But then, in a context like this, Paul gives us the seven "ones" on which Christian unity is to be based (Ephesians 4:4–6). The one faith and the one baptism are once again right together. Christians must be united because they have all responded to the one Lord with the one faith and the one baptism. This is what has brought them all into the one body in which they all share the one hope because of their relationship to the one God.

Colossians 2:11–12

> In him you were also circumcised, in the putting off
> of the sinful nature, not with a circumcision done by
> the hands of men but with the circumcision done by
> Christ, having been buried with him in baptism and
> raised with him through your faith in the power of
> God, who raised him from the dead.

The theme of Colossians is primarily the all-sufficiency of Christ; however Paul never misses an opportunity to stress the heart of the gospel. Having described the supremacy of Christ, in chapter 1 he goes on to say,

> Once you were alienated from God and were enemies
> in your minds because of your evil behavior. But now
> he has reconciled you by Christ's physical body
> through death to present you holy in his sight, with-
> out blemish and free from accusation—if you contin-
> ue in your faith, established and firm, not moved
> from the hope held out in the gospel. This is the
> gospel that you heard and that has been proclaimed
> to every creature under heaven, and of which I, Paul,
> have become a servant. (Colossians 1:21–23)

Having emphasized the gospel that incredibly positions us before God "without blemish and free from accusation" because of our faith, Paul wants to remind the Colossians of the moment in baptism when they put off the old nature and were raised with Christ "through [their] faith." Once again, we could say that faith and baptism are the inside and the outside of the same fabric—the response of someone ready to trust Christ alone.

When we look carefully at all these passages, we see that baptism is not, as is sometimes said, just a symbol. Particularly in Romans 6, Galatians 3 and Colossians 2, we see that baptism is a most significant and powerful reality. It is really a union with Christ's death, burial and resurrection. It is really a putting on of Christ. To the eyes of the world it may look like just a ceremony—even a silly ceremony, but *because of our faith* (and only because of our faith), it is an intimate union with Christ. Though a physical act, it is by its very nature a humble expression of need and trust.

It is clear that those who responded to the good news of God's grace were called to submit to Christ in baptism. Having said this, we must also insist that in baptism God is more active than we are. Baptism is not a place where we are working or, God forbid, earning our salvation. Baptism is a place where God works. It is a place where *he* forgives us and gives us the gift of his Spirit (Acts

2:38), where *he* unites us with Christ and his death and resurrection (Romans 6:3–4), and where *he* adds us to his body (1 Corinthians 12:13). It is important to note that when Paul reminds Christians they have *been baptized*, he uses the passive voice. Baptism is not really an arena where we "do" something. It is a place in time where we yield to God, who then actively does for us what we could not do for ourselves.

To summarize, God extends to us an incredible offer of grace. We accept this offer and enter into its benefits by turning away from our trust of ourselves, placing our trust in him, and expressing this by submitting to baptism—the God-ordained place and time of union with Christ. Justification is by grace through faith, with faith having a primacy that places it in a unique category, and repentance and baptism being a part of the response of faith.

Accept one another, then, just as Christ accepted you, in order to bring praise to God.

Romans 15:7

Get rid of all bitterness, rage and anger, brawling and slander, along with every form of malice. Be kind and compassionate to one another, forgiving each other, just as in Christ God forgave you.

Ephesians 4:31–32

Yet when I preach the gospel, I cannot boast, for I am compelled to preach. Woe to me if I do not preach the gospel!

1 Corinthians 9:16

chapter five

THE APPLICATION OF GRACE

Once the gospel of God's grace becomes our dominant conviction, we will be in a position to do the only thing that makes sense—relentlessly apply that message to our lives. In reality, we have already discussed the first and foremost application of grace, and that is to trust it. The grace of God as a great theological concept does little good until we put our faith in it. One theologian defined faith as "accepting the fact that we have been accepted." The first place for us to apply grace is to ourselves. This is what saving faith is all about. It is accepting our acceptance. It is trusting the fact that God's grace, which comes through Christ, has made us completely acceptable to God. It is looking at the fact that we are still sinners, but trusting that we have been translated into a state of grace where we are "holy and blameless in his sight" (Ephesians

1:4), "without blemish and free from accusation" (Colossians 1:22), "heirs of God and co-heirs with Christ" (Romans 8:17), and "a chosen people, a royal priesthood, a holy nation, a people belonging to God" (1 Peter 2:9). It has been pointed out that there are many religions who know no divine welcome for the sinner until he ceases to be one. The astounding and amazing message of the Christian gospel is that sinners such as we can be so fully accepted by God and treated as if we had never sinned at all. This why there has probably never been a song written with a more accurate title than "Amazing Grace."

But while some of us accept the theology of grace and could give the right answers about it, we do not readily apply it personally and internally. Tapes from our childhood and from our experiences in the world keep playing in our minds, telling us that we don't measure up. We know so many people who relate to us on the basis of our performance that we deeply believe this is probably the way God still relates to us. I had been preaching and teaching the gospel of God's grace for many years, but I can remember exactly where I was—actually walking through a shopping mall— when I allowed myself to say, "God really does accept you, so why don't you accept yourself?" I don't think I said it out loud. At least I don't remember any strange looks from other shoppers, but it was a booming voice inside me. This did not just come strangely out of the blue. I had been reading Romans 6–8 for several days. In my case, that experience did not mark the complete end of the struggle against guilt, but for me it was a watershed moment. From that point on, anytime the accusing tapes began to play, I could say, "No, because of Christ, I am accepted by God."

But what about those who don't deal much with accusations, those who are more "excused" than "accused"? How do they need to apply grace to their lives? Again, I would suggest that the key words are "faith" and "trust." Justification is by faith for us all. They need to trust the fact that they need grace as much as anyone else. They need to trust that without the grace of a Savior, their sins, many of which they don't even see, would cause them to be alienated from God. They need to trust that their right standing with God is not based on their wonderful personality or the way they are calm under fire, but solely on the righteousness of Christ. For them the application of grace will mean freely acknowledging how deceived they can be about who they are and how they sin, and letting others know how grateful they are for the grace of God that has both revealed and met their need.

For those who don't "feel" the need for grace as much as others, I would make two further suggestions: (1) Frequently reread the Sermon on the Mount (Matthew 5–7). I don't believe that anyone with a soft heart can hear the challenges found there and not say, "Go away from me, Lord; I am a sinful man [or woman]!" (Luke 5:8). As noted earlier, the message of that sermon (which certainly describes God's perfect will for us) will drive you again and again back to that first beatitude where you will confess your spiritual poverty. (2) Look carefully at Paul. From his statements in Philippians chapter 3 it would seem that he was quite deceived and comfortable with his own righteousness before he met Christ, but God's revelation showed him that all his righteousness and confidence in himself was dung (literally the word in Philippians 3:8). The truth is that those of you who don't "feel" as much need for grace, should be grateful that God in his grace is not blowing you off the map because of your pride, but is showing you who you really are, how much he loves you anyway and what he wants to do with you when you stop trusting yourself.

Certainly we must first personally connect with God's grace and apply it to our own lives. But when we turn to the Scriptures, the great abundance of texts speak of how we need to apply grace in our relationship with others. It is here that I believe we need to open ourselves up to much new thinking. Because we have often slipped back into a performance-based mentality, we have quite naturally begun to relate to each other on that basis. The New Testament is rife with passages calling us to show to others the same grace, unconditional love, acceptance and favor that God has shown to us.

Perhaps no teaching of Jesus illustrates this more than what we often call the "Parable of the Unmerciful Servant":

> "Therefore, the kingdom of heaven is like a king who wanted to settle accounts with his servants. As he began the settlement, a man who owed him ten thousand talents was brought to him. Since he was not able to pay, the master ordered that he and his wife and his children and all that he had be sold to repay the debt.
>
> "The servant fell on his knees before him. 'Be patient with me,' he begged, 'and I will pay back everything.'

The servant's master took pity on him, canceled the debt and let him go.

"But when that servant went out, he found one of his fellow servants who owed him a hundred denarii. He grabbed him and began to choke him. 'Pay back what you owe me!' he demanded.

"His fellow servant fell to his knees and begged him, 'Be patient with me, and I will pay you back.'

"But he refused. Instead, he went off and had the man thrown into prison until he could pay the debt. When the other servants saw what had happened, they were greatly distressed and went and told their master everything that had happened.

"Then the master called the servant in. 'You wicked servant,' he said, 'I canceled all that debt of yours because you begged me to. Shouldn't you have had mercy on your fellow servant just as I had on you?' In anger his master turned him over to the jailers to be tortured, until he should pay back all he owed.

"This is how my heavenly Father will treat each of you unless you forgive your brother from your heart." (Matthew 18:23–35)

The servant in the story owes his master a monstrous amount of money. Some have calculated that ten thousand talents would translate into something between ten and fifteen million U.S. dollars. Since servants made the equivalent of about twenty-five cents a day, it would have taken the servant well in excess of 100,000 years to pay off the debt—*if* there was no interest and *if* he could put everything he made toward the debt. We may want to know how he got in such a fix, but that

> Applying grace then means extending grace. Do others "deserve" it? No, but then neither did I.

is not the point of the story. The point is that he was desperately and hopelessly in debt. His reply is either pathetic or laughable, depending on how you look at it: "Be patient with me, and I will pay back everything."

The only thing that could save this man was grace, and that is exactly what he received. The master took pity on him, forgave the debt and let him go. Had this man possessed a shred of gratitude and the slightest understanding of applying grace, he would have understood that what had been shown to him, he now needed to show to others. But at the first opportunity to do this, he promptly forgot what had been done for him and demanded immediate payment from a man who owed him a much smaller (and a completely payable) debt. Jesus goes on to show how a failure to "pass along" grace means that we forfeit its value in our lives. If we do not let grace transform us, we demonstrate that we are putting no faith in it at all. We are simply using it selfishly, and we are not trusting it.

As I apply this parable to my life, I understand that I am the ten-million-dollar debtor who has been forgiven, and anything someone else does to me is but a fifteen-dollar-debt in comparison to the enormous burden that God has removed from my life. *Applying grace* then means *extending grace.* Do others "deserve" it? No, but then neither did I. Grace by its very nature is not giving others what they do deserve—probably judgment—but instead giving them what they do not deserve—forgiveness and acceptance. And, I would add, not feeling the least bit self-righteous when we do this, as we are only showing others what God has so generously shown us.

There are plenty of other places in the New Testament where Christian ethics are discussed in terms of treating others with the grace with which

God has treated us. Consider the following examples:

> "You have heard that it was said, 'Love your neighbor and hate your enemy.' But I tell you: Love your enemies and pray for those who persecute you, that you may be sons of your Father in heaven. He causes his sun to rise on the evil and the good, and sends rain on the righteous and the unrighteous. If you love those who love you, what reward will you get? Are not even the tax collectors doing that?" (Matthew 5:43–46)

> Accept one another, then, just as Christ accepted you, in order to bring praise to God. (Romans 15:7)

> Now this is our boast: Our conscience testifies that we have conducted ourselves in the world, and especially in our relations with you, in the holiness and sincerity that are from God. We have done so not according to worldly wisdom but according to God's grace. (2 Corinthians 1:12)

> Get rid of all bitterness, rage and anger, brawling and slander, along with every form of malice. Be kind and compassionate to one another, forgiving each other, just as in Christ God forgave you. (Ephesians 4:31–32)

Be imitators of God, therefore, as dearly loved children and live a life of love, just as Christ loved us and gave himself up for us as a fragrant offering and sacrifice to God. (Ephesians 5:1–2)

Therefore, as God's chosen people, holy and dearly loved, clothe yourselves with compassion, kindness, humility, gentleness and patience. Bear with each other and forgive whatever grievances you may have against one another. Forgive as the Lord forgave you. (Colossians 3:12–13)

This is how God showed his love among us: He sent his one and only Son into the world that we might live through him. This is love: not that we loved God, but that he loved us and sent his Son as an atoning sacrifice for our sins. Dear friends, since God so loved us, we also ought to love one another. (1 John 4:9–11)

All of these passages make clear that the way God demonstrates grace toward us must then be the way we demonstrate grace toward others. Paul said it this way to Titus: "The grace of God teaches us...." The way God has treated us by extending such costly grace (let us never forget that the price was the precious blood of Jesus), is teaching and training us to relate to others the same way. We will only receive grace if we are humble enough to confess how much we need it, but that same humility will lead us to eagerly learn to show the same grace to others (or at least listen to others who can help us see how we are not showing grace to them).

My friend and fellow elder Wyndham Shaw recently spoke about forgiving as the Lord has forgiven you from Colossians 3:13. He pointed us back to Colossians 1:22 and reminded us that when God forgives, there is no more accusation. Extending grace means I forgive you and no longer accuse you. I certainly hold nothing against you. His message was a reminder to me of how many facets God's forgiveness has—how thorough it is, how promptly it comes, and how completely it embraces.

It is unthinkable to talk about the application of grace without talking about how the receiving of it places on us a responsibility to tell others about it. If we have been so blessed and so privileged to have this message made plain to us so that we might respond and be reconciled to God, how could we hold this truth back from others who need it just as much as we do? I would suggest that this understanding is what was at work in Paul when he wrote the following words to the Romans and to the Corinthians (emphasis is added):

> *I am obligated* both to Greeks and non-Greeks, both to the wise and the foolish. That is *why I am so eager* to preach the gospel also to you who are at Rome.
>
> *I am not ashamed* of the gospel, because it is the power of God for the salvation of everyone who believes: first for the Jew, then for the Gentile. (Romans 1:14–16)
>
> Yet when I preach the gospel, I cannot boast, for *I am compelled to preach. Woe to me if I do not preach the gospel!* If I preach voluntarily, I have a reward; if not voluntarily, I am simply discharging the trust committed to me. What then is my reward? Just this: that in preaching the gospel I may offer it free of charge, and so not make use of my rights in preaching it. (1 Corinthians 9:16–18)
>
> If we are out of our mind, it is for the sake of God; if we are in our right mind, it is for you. *For Christ's love compels us,* because we are convinced that one died for all, and therefore all died. And he died for

all, that those who live should no longer live for themselves but for him who died for them and was raised again. (2 Corinthians 5:13–15)

Paul felt obligated and compelled to pass this message on, not because he thought he needed to fill a quota to somehow secure his own salvation. He felt the obligation and compulsion that come from gratitude. A friend of mine told a story about something that happened many years ago when his now-grown son was only a small boy. One day while walking on a downtown street, his son ran into a plate glass window at a store, breaking the window and severing a major artery. An off-duty policeman rushed to his aid and held his hand on the severed artery all the way the hospital, saving his life. So grateful for this act, my friend went to the police station the next week and volunteered to do anything they might need done. He was compelled by gratitude.

Applying grace to our lives will produce gratitude, and that same heart that sacrificed to reach out to us will begin to beat in our own breasts. Even if there had been no Great Commission, the grace of God would be great enough to commission us to tell the world around us.

I do not think that the churches I am most closely associated with have spent nearly enough time discussing the implications of grace or the application of grace to a wide variety of issues and situations, but I am heartened by how many are now opening themselves to these considerations. All such efforts, carefully guided by Scripture, will only result in our being a healthier people.

It is by applying grace that we become the light of the world and the salt of the earth. It is through applying grace that we "will make the teaching of God our Savior attractive" (Titus 2:10).

What shall we say, then? Shall we go on sinning so that grace may increase? By no means! We died to sin; how can we live in it any longer? Or don't you know that all of us who were baptized into Christ Jesus were baptized into his death? We were therefore buried with him through baptism into death in order that, just as Christ was raised from the dead through the glory of the Father, we too may live a new life.

Romans 6:1–4

For the grace of God that brings salvation has appeared to all men. It teaches us to say "No" to ungodliness and worldly passions, and to live self-controlled, upright and godly lives in this present age....

Titus 2:11–12

THE ABUSE OF GRACE

Since man, by nature, has a deceitful heart (Jeremiah 17:9), we can be sure that he will often take something good from God and abuse it or misuse it. It is hard to think of any Biblical doctrine that has not been misused by somebody. So we should expect that people will try to "take advantage" of the sound teaching on grace, primarily by using it as a license to do as they please. As Paul and other New Testament writers proclaimed the gospel of God's grace, they were well aware of this tendency. The little book of Jude contains one of the strongest and clearest warnings in this regard:

> For certain men whose condemnation was written about long ago have secretly slipped in among you. They are godless men, who change the grace of our God into a license for immorality and deny Jesus Christ our only Sovereign and Lord. (Jude 1:4)

In his second letter, it seems Peter is referring to some with the same grace-abusing tendencies when he writes about those who have come to know Christ, but in the name of freedom are once again wallowing in the mud:

> These men are springs without water and mists driven by a storm. Blackest darkness is reserved for them. For they mouth empty, boastful words and, by appealing to the lustful desires of sinful human nature, they entice people who are just escaping from those who live in error. They promise them freedom, while they themselves are slaves of depravity—for a man is a slave to whatever has mastered him. If they have escaped the corruption of the world by knowing our Lord and Savior Jesus Christ and are again entangled in it and overcome, they are worse off at the end than they were at the beginning. It would have been better for them not to have known the way of righteousness, than to have known it and then to turn their backs on the sacred command that was passed on to them. Of them the proverbs are true: "A dog returns to its vomit," and, "A sow that is washed goes back to her wallowing in the mud." (2 Peter 2:17–22)

We have already seen Paul address this potential abuse in Romans 6. I especially like the J. B. Phillips translation of Romans 6:1–2: "Now what is our response to be? Shall we sin to our heart's content and see how far we can exploit the grace of God? What a ghastly thought!" To the Galatians, Paul preaches and exalts freedom in Christ, but he rounds out his message to them by saying, "You, my brothers, were called to be free. But do not use your freedom to indulge the sinful nature; rather, serve one another in love" (Galatians 5:13). He goes on to warn them, "The acts of the sinful nature are obvious...; those who do such things will not inherit the kingdom of God" (Galatians 5:19–21). And finally,

> **Far from being a license to sin, the grace of God is what shows us how to live.**

> Do not be deceived: God cannot be mocked. A man reaps what he sows. The one who sows to please his sinful nature, from that nature will reap destruction; the one who sows to please the Spirit, from the Spirit will reap eternal life. (Galatians 6:7–8)

Far from being a license to sin, the grace of God is what shows us how to live. This is the import of one of the verses from Titus that we looked at as we began this study:

> For the grace of God that brings salvation has appeared to all men. It teaches us to say "No" to ungodliness and worldly passions, and to live self-controlled, upright and godly lives in this present age.... (Titus 2:11–12)

As we put the gospel of grace at the very heart of our message, we will always need to teach that it does not mean a freedom to return to sin. If that is what it meant, the grace of God would have been offered in vain. God's grace has come to free us from the slavery of sin, to empower us to live a new life. To use it as an excuse to return to an old and meaningless life would be the worst of follies, not to mention the height of ingratitude. Peter's picture of the dog going back to his vomit and the sow returning to the mud should be indelibly painted on our minds.

But here is where we must be careful. The fact that people have abused the teaching of grace and will always try to do so, must never become a reason for us not to proclaim it as the heart of our message. People will misuse the teaching of commitment and obedience and submission, but we must not back away from teaching what is Biblical—on any subject. We must not base our message on reactions to what people have done, but rather, on the clear call of Scripture.

We must proclaim the grace of God and always keep it at the center of our teaching. Then we can be concerned about guarding against dangers on the left and on the right. On one side will be those who will foolishly try to use the grace of God as an excuse or a pass. On the other side will be another human tendency to move away from the grace model and to move toward the performance model. We must recognize that this model is always trying to make a comeback, especially among those who see themselves as zealous for God. With both dangers equally threatening, it will take consistent commitment to keep the gospel of grace in its rightful place. That is probably why Paul told Timothy, "Guard the good deposit that was entrusted to you" (2 Timothy 1:14). The precious and trustworthy message must be protected. It will, however, be well worth any effort to be uncompromising in our proclamation of the gospel of God's grace.

I have been crucified with Christ and I no longer live, but Christ lives in me. The life I live in the body, I live by faith in the Son of God, who loved me and gave himself for me.

Galatians 2:20

What is more, I consider everything a loss compared to the surpassing greatness of knowing Christ Jesus my Lord, for whose sake I have lost all things. I consider them rubbish, that I may gain Christ and be found in him, not having a righteousness of my own that comes from the law, but that which is through faith in Christ—the righteousness that comes from God and is by faith.

Philippians 3:8–9

chapter  seven

GRACE, FAITH AND DISCIPLESHIP

When we put the proper emphasis on justification by grace through faith, how should we think about discipleship? The way some of us have studied the Bible with people has often left the impression that you are saved by becoming a disciple and that being a disciple means that you do x, y, z. This can certainly leave the impression with people that they are saved through their own efforts. In our desire to stress some of Jesus' strong teachings, we can get out on a limb, far from the trunk of the tree. However, with grace in clear view, how should we think about discipleship?

When some of us hear the word "discipleship," we immediately think more of what has been called "discipling"—a term used by a variety of religious groups to describe the horizontal relationships we have with each other as we seek to mature each other in Christ. That is both a legitimate aspect of discipleship and a practice that has sometimes been abused. We must not let the presence of the latter cause us to reject the former. The New Testament clearly calls us to be involved in each other's lives, helping each other to guard our hearts (Hebrews 3:12–13) and bringing each other encouragement and correction (Colossians 3:16 and others). However, when I use the term here, I use it first to mean the lifestyle that comes from the serious decision to be a disciple of Jesus. I am talking more about your vertical relationship with Christ than your horizontal relationship with others, though I would not want to draw too sharp a distinction between the two.

Is 'Discipleship' Still a Valid Term?

First of all, it has been suggested by some that the whole concept of discipleship no longer applies to us who do not live in the presence of the physical Jesus. One writer has expressed this opinion on a Web posting:

> Simply stated, it seems that New Testament discipleship had to do with physically following a physical Messiah. Once that Messiah went to heaven, discipleship was not possible (since

discipleship by definition involves the physical following of a physical teacher). Belief was a far more applicable concept, and "believers" became one of the most popular terms of identification for Christians in the church age. Our theology and practice seem to fail to recognize the fact that the term "disciple" faded from use in the apostolic church, only appearing rarely in Acts and never again in the New Testament.

While I respect and appreciate the many thoughtful articles I have read from the author of this statement, I cannot accept this view for two reasons. First, the gospels were written later in the first century, at least as late as some of Paul's letters and in some cases later. These documents were written to the churches, just as were the letters, and they were written to remind Christians of what Jesus taught about following him. The Christians (probably in Rome) who received Mark's gospel needed to hear that Jesus said to anyone who would come after him, "You must deny yourself, take up the cross and follow me." Mark's gospel is not just a journalist's account of what Jesus said and did. It is a presentation of the message of Jesus for the church, most likely in the midst of persecution. It is quite probable that none of these Christians in Rome had ever been with the physical Jesus, but they still needed to hear the message of what it meant to come to Jesus and learn from him.

Second, and more decisively, disciples are referred to twenty-eight times in the book of Acts, and those references are not confined to the early chapters. It really cannot be said that the word "disciple" is rare in the book of Acts. More importantly, after Jesus had resurrected and ascended, Luke tells us that "the number of disciples was increasing" (Acts 6:1) and "the number of disciples… increased rapidly" (Acts 6:7). It was no longer possible to follow the physical Jesus around Palestine, but the number of people who were becoming disciples was increasing rapidly. The message of Jesus had spread to Antioch after the persecution following the death of Stephen (Acts 11:19). Some years later, Saul and Barnabas came there to strengthen the church, and Luke tells us that "for a whole year Barnabas and Saul met with the church and taught great numbers of people. *The disciples were called Christians* first at Antioch" (Acts 11:26, emphasis added). In a city hundreds of miles from where Jesus lived and long after people could be with him physically, those who were believing in his message and putting their faith in him were called disciples, and those people eventually took the name Christians (even though it was probably put on them in derision).

Some time later Paul and Barnabas traveled on to Asia Minor, yet Luke continues to use the same terminology. "They preached the good news in that city and *won a large number of disciples.* Then they returned to Lystra, Iconium and Antioch...." (Acts 14:21, emphasis added). If Paul and Barnabas on another continent, many years after the ascension of Jesus into heaven, can still be winning *"a large number of disciples,"* that would seem to settle the issue. There is no reason to think that the idea of being a disciple was in any way limited to those who could physically be with Jesus. You can say that it is interesting that believers are not called disciples in the letters, but there is no reason to argue that the term is no longer a good one for us. I think it is wise for us not to use any one term (like "disciple") exclusively when there are many other Biblical ways to refer to followers of Jesus. However, I don't see a reason for us to discontinue the use of the term "disciple" just as it was used in many places in Asia and Europe (Acts 14:28, 15:10, 16:1, 18:23, 18:27, 19:1,19:9, 21:4, 21:16).

Before his ascension, Jesus told his followers to go and make disciples. He was physically leaving, but the making of disciples was to continue "to the very end of the age" (Matthew 28:18–20). We see in Acts that they took this charge seriously.

Grace and Discipleship

Now back to the question of grace, faith and discipleship. Clearly in Acts the grace of God was being preached, and people were being taught that they would be saved as they believed or put their faith in that message. Paul, on one occasion, describes Jesus' message to him:

> "I will rescue you from your own people and from the Gentiles. I am sending you to them to open their eyes and turn them from darkness to light, and from the power of Satan to God, *so that they may receive forgiveness of sins and a place among those who are sanctified by faith in me.*" (Acts 26:17–18, emphasis added)

It was Jesus who had taught Paul about sanctification by faith, and that was the message Paul preached. Those who responded to that message were called "believers" (thirteen times in Acts) but they were also called disciples (again, twenty-eight times). To repent and turn to God, to put your faith in the message and work of Jesus, was to become a disciple. It was to become one who was now ready to learn from Jesus and one who was eager to submit to him.

In two of his great letters that deal with justification by grace through faith, Paul describes our response to grace in ways that line up completely with what Jesus taught about being a disciple. To the Galatians, Paul said, "I have been crucified with Christ and I no longer live, but Christ lives in me. The life I live in the body, I live by faith in the Son of God, who loved me and gave himself for me" (Galatians 2:20). The Greek here literally says "I have been co-crucified with Christ." Putting faith in Jesus means denying yourself and taking up the cross. It means dying to all efforts at self-justification and all efforts to control your own life. To live by faith in the Son of God means to say, "I no longer live, but Christ lives in me." Later on, to the Galatians, Paul will say, "Those who belong to Christ Jesus have crucified the sinful nature with its passions and desires" (Galatians 5:24). Those who have trusted in the grace of Christ will continue to talk about taking up the cross and will continue to get on it.

In the midst of some great chapters to the Romans that show salvation is by grace through faith, Paul will write three times in chapter 6 that those who have believed and have been baptized have "died with Christ" (vv2, 7 and 8). That is who a disciple is—one who has said, "My old life needs to be denied (disowned) and needs to be crucified with Christ." The person who dies with Christ in baptism is the person who is raised to a new life. Paul's message is the same as that of Jesus, who said, "For whoever wants to save his life will lose it, but whoever loses his life for me will find it" (Matthew 16:25). When we die with Christ, we are raised to life that is real. That is discipleship. Just as the concept of grace is all through the gospels though Jesus never personally uses the word, the concept of discipleship is all through the letters, even though Paul does not use the word.

Having written in many ways about the grace of God in the first eleven chapters of Romans, Paul begins chapter 12 with these words: "Therefore, I urge you, brothers, *in view of God's mercy, to offer your bodies as living sacrifices,* holy and pleasing to God—this is your spiritual act of worship" (Romans 12:1, emphasis added). What is the only appropriate response to the grace of God? It is to offer yourself completely to God—putting your whole self on the altar. Is this not the same as Jesus' message: "In the same way, any of you who does not give up everything he has cannot be my disciple" (Luke 14:33). Both passages are for us today.

> Those who have trusted in the grace of Christ will continue to talk about taking up the cross and will continue to get on it.

There is nothing about the message of grace and salvation through faith in grace that undermines or negates the message of discipleship. Describing the true grace of God, Bonhoeffer wrote, "Such grace is *costly* because it calls us to follow, and *it is grace* because it calls us to follow Jesus Christ. It is *costly* because it costs a man his life, and *it is grace* because it gives a man the only true life. It is *costly* because it condemns sin, and *it is grace* because it justifies the sinner."[1]

If we have taught people that they will be saved only after they have performed certain actions of a disciple, then we must change. We could never do

---

[1]Dietrich Bonhoeffer, *The Cost of Discipleship* (New York: Touchstone, 1995) 45.

enough as a disciple to bring about the forgiveness of even one sin, much less justify ourselves and accomplish salvation. But if we are teaching people that in view of the mercy of God, they should offer themselves as living sacrifices, then we are on the mark. If we are teaching them that "love so amazing, so divine, demands my soul, my life, my all," we are proclaiming grace and truth.

We must be careful that we never teach "salvation by discipleship," as I believe some have. Salvation is by grace through faith. However, we must make it clear that a thankful acceptance of grace must be linked with a heart that desires to be transformed into the image of Christ. How can it not be?

Perhaps no passage brings the message of righteousness by grace through faith and the heart of discipleship together better than this one from Philippians:

> What is more, *I consider everything a loss* compared to the surpassing greatness of knowing Christ Jesus my Lord, for whose sake I have lost all things. I consider them rubbish, that I may gain Christ and be found in him, *not having a righteousness of my own that comes from the law, but that which is through faith in Christ*—the righteousness that comes from

God and is by faith. *I want to know Christ* and the power of his resurrection and the fellowship of sharing in his sufferings, becoming like him in his death, and so, somehow, to attain to the resurrection from the dead....

All of us who are mature should take such a view of things. And if on some point you think differently, that too God will make clear to you. (Philippians 3:8–11, 15, emphasis added)

If we restore the emphasis on the gospel of God's grace, will there be the need to call people to be disciples? Absolutely. He who was "full of grace" called anyone who would come after him to deny himself, take up the cross and follow him. The grace of God has come so that we might become disciples, so we might follow Jesus, so we might live a new life in which we are becoming like him (Romans 8:28–29, 2 Corinthians 3:18). Again, in the words of Bonhoeffer, "Cheap grace is the preaching of forgiveness without repentance, baptism without church discipline, communion without confession. *Cheap grace is grace without discipleship,* grace without the cross, grace without Jesus Christ, living and incarnate."[2] In our day we must be committed

---

[2] Bonhoeffer, 44–45, emphasis added.

to "testifying to the gospel of God's grace" (Acts 20:24), to proclaiming "the whole will of God" (Acts 20:27) and to praying that the number of disciples might increase (Acts 6:1).

I am not ashamed of the gospel, because it is the power of God for the salvation of everyone who believes: first for the Jew, then for the Gentile.

Romans 1:16

c o n c l u s i o n

THE POWER OF THE GOSPEL

Writing to the Romans, Paul said, "I am not ashamed of the gospel, because it is the power of God for the salvation of everyone who believes: first for the Jew, then for the Gentile. For in the gospel a righteousness from God is revealed, a righteousness that is by faith from first to last, just as it is written: 'The righteous will live by faith'" (Romans 1:16–17). The message of God's grace that comes to us through Christ is truly an amazing message! When it is received, the power of God is released in people's lives. We have much to learn about the application of the message of grace, but everything we learn brings more power to our lives.

If you have never renounced your confidence in your own righteousness and placed your trust in the sacrifice of Christ, I pray you will seriously look at who he is and what this means. I pray that the things you have read here will encourage you to turn to him in repentance and to be united with him in baptism.

If you have always believed in God's grace but have allowed other messages to take priority over it, I pray you will become "strong in the grace" and let the message of what God has done be the passion of your life. The gospel of God's grace is not the only message we should be passionate about, but without emphasis on this grace, our passion for other themes may very well do more harm than good.

Putting the good news of God's grace at the center of our message will not fix all problems in the church. The grace of God was at the center of the message in the first century, and there were still problems. I am not suggesting that this is a panacea for all that ails us. What I am saying is that we have no hope of being healthy unless we are passionate about this trustworthy message. As we address any problem in the church, it must be from the foundation of God's grace.

As we evaluate who we are and where we are going, may God raise up a multitude of souls who will say with Paul, "However, I consider my life worth nothing to me, if only I may finish the race and complete the task the Lord Jesus has given me—the task of testifying to the gospel of God's grace" (Acts 20:24).

THE GRACE OF GOD: A STUDY

*The following is an example of a Bible study that could be done
with someone you are seeking to bring to Christ.*

1. **2 Corinthians 5:10**—Do you feel confident about stand-
    ing before the judgment seat of Christ? Why or why not? In
    this study we will learn how we can be completely confi-
    dent about standing before God.

2. There are more than 110 specific references to the grace
    of God in the New Testament and many other times when
    the concept is alluded to. Grace is a major biblical theme.

    A. **Acts 14:26**—What does "the grace of God" mean to
        you?
    B. **Acts 20:24**—Why was the message of Jesus called
        "the gospel of God's grace"?

3. There are two basic ways that people could be saved (be
    accepted by God):

    A. **Works model**—Earning our place with God by doing
        all the right things.
        1) Here the standard is perfection.
            a) **James 2:10**—To even fail at one point is to
                be guilty of all. One sin would keep one
                from being saved by works.
            b) **Galatians 5:3**—Written to those taking *cer-
                tain* works and making them the standard
                for salvation.

    c) **Romans 3:23**—Based on works, what is everyone's situation?

  2) If God made anything less than perfection acceptable, where do you think he should draw the line? 95%, 90%, 80%, 65%? How fair would God be to save the person who made a 65 on the morality-and-works scale and condemn the person just a point behind at 64? God can have only one performance standard—perfection!

B. **Grace model**—God giving us salvation as a gift that we have not earned and do not deserve.

  1) Here your perfection or performance is not the issue. The issue is what Christ has done and how you respond to him.

    a) **Romans 3:22–25a**—"Justified" (declared not guilty) freely by his grace.

    b) **Romans 4:4–8**—Why is the person who comes to Christ totally saved? (Because the righteousness of Christ is "credited" to his or her account.)

    c) **Colossians 1:21–23**—How does God view a person who has been reconciled to him through Christ? "Holy...without blemish and free from accusation"! Is such a one really without blemish? Why does God view him or her this way?

  2) This grace was made available only because Jesus was willing to pay the enormous price that had to be paid for sin.

    a) **2 Corinthians 8:9**—He became poor for our sakes.

b) **Hebrews 2:9**—He experienced death for all men.

c) **1 Peter 1:18–19**—We are redeemed, not with perishable things, but with the precious blood of Christ.

d) **1 John 5:8–10**—What does all this mean? (God loves us! He loved us so much he sent Jesus to die for our sins so we might be saved by grace!)

4. If salvation is not by works but by grace, is everyone saved?

A. **Hebrews 2:9**—Who did Jesus die for?

B. **1 Timothy 2:3–5**—How many does God want saved?

C. **2 Thessalonians 1:6–10**—Are all people going to be saved? If Jesus died for all and wants to give grace to all, but not all are going to be saved, what does that tell us?

1) We must accept his offer. We must receive the pardon. We must say "Yes, I want the relationship with God that comes by grace."

2) Illustration: A pardon that is not accepted does not become a pardon.

D. **Acts 2:36–39**

1) How did Peter tell his listeners to accept the grace of God?

a) Repentance—turning to Christ and away from the world.

b) Baptism—giving God your old life to bury, so by grace he can raise up a new life.

2) What gifts did he promise that God would freely give?

      a)   Forgiveness of sins—because we have trusted in what Jesus did.

      b)   The Holy Spirit—to help us live the new life.

5.   Who can be *completely confident* about his or her salvation?

   A.   The person who has accepted God's grace just as these people did in Acts 2.

   B.   The person who keeps his or her faith in Jesus and never leaves him.

   C.   **Colossians 1:22–23, Hebrews 3:14**
       Confidence rests on what Jesus has done. If we are responding in faith to him, it is his work that saves us—not our own performance. Our performance will vary. His work of salvation never does. He redeems us. He justifies us. He reconciles us. We are secure.

6.   What is the only right response to "salvation by grace"?

   A.   **1 John 3:1**—Rejoicing and amazement.

   B.   **1 Corinthians 15:9–10**—Total commitment to Jesus.

7.   Have you accepted God's grace? Are you saved by his grace?

For help in applying grace in a more personal
and practical way in your life, watch for
an upcoming new release from DPI:
The Guilty Soul's Guide to Grace by Sam Laing.

NOTES

NOTES

NOTES

WHO ARE WE?

Discipleship Publications International (DPI) began publishing in 1993. We are a nonprofit Christian publisher committed to publishing and distributing materials that honor God, lift up Jesus Christ and show how his message practically applies to all areas of life. We have a deep conviction that no one changes life like Jesus and that the implementation of his teaching will revolutionize any life, any marriage, any family and any singles household.

Since our beginning, we have published more than 130 titles; plus, we have produced a number of helpful audio products. More than two million volumes have been printed, and our works have been translated into more than a dozen languages—international is not just a part of our name! Our books are shipped regularly to every inhabited continent.

To see a more detailed description of our works, find us on the World Wide Web at www.dpibooks.org. You can order books by calling 1-888-DPI-BOOK seven days a week, twenty-four hours a day. From outside the US, call 419-281-1802.

We appreciate the hundreds of comments we have received from readers. We would love to hear from you. Here are other ways to get in touch:

Mail: DPI, 2 Sterling Road, Billerica, Mass. 01862-2595
E-Mail: dpibooks@icoc.org

Find Us on the World Wide Web
www.dpibooks.org

1-888-DPI-BOOK
Outside the US
Call 419-281-1802